The 6 Pillars of Self Esteem for Teens

Help Teens to Overcome Insecurity, Self-Acceptance, Inside Fears and Controlling Negative Thoughts

By

Harvey Paul

ASH Publisher

About the Author

Harvey Paul is a well-known name in the world of e-books regarding teen mindset-related concerns. The author has extensive knowledge in this field and is skilled at making a quick impression on readers. He is an expert in teaching teens growth mindsets. The most effective advice and methods for removing entrenched attitudes. His writings guarantee that the readers will receive the high-quality and latest information. To empower teenagers to take care of themselves, Harvey makes sure to write useful and solution-focused books.

Table of Contents

Introduction

Do you judge yourself based on a single incident?

Do you presume that there is nothing you can do to alter the situation?

Do you pay attention to what others think of you?

Everyone wants to feel confident about themselves. We want to feel important when we wake up in the morning. We all want to feel appreciated and think of ourselves as valuable.

A person can experience disappointment and sadness if they lack an important part of their personality which is "Self-Esteem". Also if they lack sufficient self-belief and self-confidence, which are both deeply linked to self-esteem, such people may never achieve anything bigger in their practical life.

Most of us chase these feelings throughout our lives in varying situations such as, when we acquire something specific that we have desired for long, when a person in our life supports us unexpectedly, or when we achieve a specific goal. We have faith that things will improve and we will eventually feel confident in ourselves. These feelings are problematic because they shift our control of self to others. They make us dependent on others, specific events, or destiny to be happy. They keep us chasing after the sense of self-worth we're looking for, but we are rarely able to capture them.

Happiness starts with your own self. Not with your job, your relationships, or how much money you have, but with you!

You could feel isolated and alone while dealing with issues like stress or depression. Yet you most certainly are not. There are numerous other people of all ages, out there who are dealing with similar problems. Regardless of their age or how they may appear, behave, or show themselves to the outer world, most people struggle with low self-esteem. It might not be easy to believe, but this is real.

People with healthy self-esteem have good power of decision-making, good mental health and good relationships with others. Self-esteem affects all aspects of life, including friendships, mental well-being and overall health. It also has great effects on teens' motivation since those with strong, balanced self-esteem are aware of their abilities and may be motivated to confront new challenges.

As the author of this book, I want to narrate my story. When I was a teenager, I used to mistrust my decision-making power, and doubted my capabilities to achieve something bigger for myself. I was always very much dependent on someone else's approval. I even faced bullying in my school days, due to this lack of self-esteem. I didn't know how to be confident enough so that no one would take me for granted. But when I learned about the importance and benefits of self-esteem from my teacher, I realized that many good things have already happened in my life. So, from that moment onwards, I committed to educating teenagers about this essential personality trait.

This book will assist you with more than just improving your self-esteem; it will also help you to overcome your insecurities, increase your feelings of self-acceptance and help you to overcome your inner fears. It will also help you to control the negative thoughts that everyone faces, especially the teenagers.

Chapter 1: Understanding Self-Esteem

How you see and regard yourself is a measure of your self-esteem. It depends on your views and perceptions about yourselves, which can occasionally seem very challenging to modify. Moreover, self-esteem is a person's real perception of their worth. It basically expresses how you feel about yourself. It may include a variety of things, including your shared identity, degree of trust in yourself, sense of achievement and feeling of connection. Lack of self-esteem can be a very serious issue because it is crucial for different aspects of life. Self-esteem entails more than just the feeling of love for yourself but is generally positive overall. It also involves believing that you deserve affection and placing importance on your ideas, feelings, beliefs, pursuits, and objectives.

"Self-esteem is the best outfit, Rock in it, Own it"

Suppose you may hear someone claiming that, "You are too slow to achieve anything." You may believe him thinking that, "He's correct. I don't possess the necessary skills." You'll feel horrible about yourself since you selected that thought. Nevertheless, you can hear the same remarks and may not take them seriously. You might think, "He doesn't know what potential I have." I have the desire and ability to accomplish amazing things! and you'll feel really good about yourself because you opted for that thought.

1.1: Positive Self-Esteem and Inherent Value

Teenagers with high positive self-esteem have a tendency to experiment, take calculated risks, and work through issues. In turn, their education and growth will be beneficial and prepare them for a happy and prosperous life. Positive self-esteem often decreases during toddlerhood and rises during adolescence and adulthood until a rather steady and long-lasting level is attained. Hence, self-esteem modifies individual characteristics across time.

Knowing your value will enable you to survive life's unavoidable storm while also enjoying the happy days. The acknowledgment of one's inherent value also underlines our connections to one another and our basic ethics. This knowledge can contribute to the development of an empathetic mindset. The quote by Hugh Downs that best captures the situation is, *"To claim my destiny is not bound to your destiny is like claiming that your side of the ship is drowning."*

Your level of self-esteem may be enhanced by:

> ✓ *Recognizing your strengths and positive qualities.*
> ✓ *Respecting and appreciating yourself as an individual.*
> ✓ *Making yourself capable of taking decisions and expressing yourself.*
> ✓ *Allowing yourself to experiment with new or challenging things.*
> ✓ *Being gentle with yourself, and keep moving on from past failures without unjustly criticizing yourself.*
> ✓ *Prioritizing to spend the time you want for yourself.*
> ✓ *Understanding that you are valued and deserving of love.*

1.2: Causes of Low Self-Esteem

Someone might have an extremely unbalanced perspective of themselves and question their skills or capabilities if they feel insecure and have low self-esteem. Relations, career and academic performance can all suffer from low self-esteem and lack of self-assurance. Without measures, it might also be damaging to their mental and physical well-being.

A person's feelings and coping mechanisms impact how people think about themselves. Teenagers' low self-esteem is most frequently caused by:

✓ *Friends who are bad influencers, non-supportive family members, or other significant people in their lives*
✓ *Assault or violence*
✓ *Low academic performance*
✓ *Abnormalities of the mood, including anxiety*
✓ *Harassment, loneliness, or stress*
✓ *Ongoing health problems*
✓ *Worry about your looks and body appearance*

1.3: Signs of Low Self-Esteem in Teens

Everyone has different factors that influence their sense of self-worth. It may be challenging to identify how you think and make adjustments if your self-esteem has exhibited some changes or has been low for some time.

Lack of Confidence

Lack of confidence may be influenced by low self-esteem, but low confidence may also aggravate or result in lowering the self-esteem. It can be beneficial to learn how to boost your self-assurance and competence. One strategy you may harness to increase self-confidence is learning and practicing new abilities.

Lack of Responsibility

Low self-esteem sufferers frequently believe that they have little obligation to their own lives or fate. This may result from their perception that they have limited power to alter the environment or themselves They may believe that they can do nothing to solve their complications.

Fear and Insecurity

People with poor self-esteem frequently fear that they have made the wrong decision even after making it. They frequently mistrust their judgment and may resist societal pressure rather than stand by their decisions. For those with low self-esteem, this can frequently result in much self-questioning and self-doubt, making it tougher for them to make important life choices.

Fear of Failing

People with low self-esteem mistrust their capacity to succeed because they lack trust in their skills. Even though they may be afraid of failing, they frequently hold back from difficulties or give up easily without giving it their full.

1.4: Building Your Own Self-Esteem: The Six Pillars

A founder in the creation of the theory supporting self-esteem was the psychotherapist and educator Nathaniel Branden. His most detailed book, "The Six Pillars of Self Esteem," contains the theories on which he spent more than seven decades on formulating these. The topic of self-esteem was never more crucial or hard to address than it is now. To develop exceptional self-esteem, there are several definitions and short methods available. The chapters in this book explain the six pillars of self-esteem in a very brief and easy to understand manner. Since we seem to be more sensitive to words of encouragement when we don't feel good about ourselves, it might be difficult to boost self-esteem at a time when we really need it. So, even if receiving praises cause you any discomfort momentarily, make it an aim for yourselves to accept them.

Chapter 2: Pillar 1: "Appreciate Your Strength; Your Self-Esteem is in Your Control"

Individuality refers to human attributes and behaviors that set them apart from each other. Without a feeling of individuality, it is challenging for someone to create their specific identity in the outside world and comprehend the key role they can perform.

Teenagers have a strong need for individuality, which becomes more important as they age. Teenagers rarely get the opportunity to share their unique sense of individuality because their life is mostly dependent on their families. Teenagers, however, have a higher urge to develop their individuality within their families and social groups.

Always be yourself; no one is Better than You!

2.1: Identify Your Priceless Intrinsic Value

Color scheme behavior charts were first taught to my son at school. I never used behavior or task sheets at home, as I intended my son to grow up with an inner motivation for helping others, contributing to the society and working hard. Intrinsic value is an idea of a positive mindset, which holds that our skills are not and that we can learn from our failures and evolve better. A degree of self-belief is also linked to intrinsic value. Generally speaking, teenagers must:

✓ Want to perform well because performing well seems wonderful. Not because it's a part of a certain competition or for a prize.
✓ Have a feeling of achievement, whether it be through their behavior or the academic performance.
✓ Recognize that everybody makes bad decisions and has rough days.
✓ Always have the ability to pick themselves up after falling down and start afresh.
✓ Always have confidence and faith in their talents.

2.2: Your Individuality Matters

Individuality is the concept of someone's sense of self-identity and how they identify their principles, ideas and place in the world. Self-esteem is built on individuality during youth. A teen's personality is the product of various social and cultural parameters and are established by external factors beyond the teen's control, such as friends, families, schools, cultural background and other social contexts, even though teenagers have some power over how those factors develop. For example, if a student is a famous football player at his school who seems to have a huge fan base and has kept his individualism, all other students will likely behave similarly to fit in. Today's youth just wants to blend in, not stick out.

The greatest achievement is being able to be who you are in a world that is constantly attempting to transform you into something else!

The fact that every creature is original and creative is arguably the most attractive and remarkable blessing to humanity. Moreover, a teenager's individuality is not dependent on his parents' convenience, choice, acceptance, or permission. The teenager must bravely fight to locate, identify and possibly believe in his identity and independence. When you understand your individual value you will realize that:

✓ *You are a different personality from other just like the fingerprints. You have the chance to develop your uniqueness throughout your lifetime.*

✓ *Your uniqueness is important for your life's main objectives and achievements. When you will achieve your goal, you will automatically understand your individual value.*

✓ *You do not need to represent anyone else. You were created to be you. Love your uniqueness and glow.*

✓ *Every day, take a glance in the mirror and celebrate your uniqueness.*

Chapter 3: Pillar 2: "Don't Let Other People Insecurities, Feelings or Viewpoints Disturb You"

All of us approach our insecurities in various ways. It could be viewed positively by certain people while negatively by the others. In the book "Teen Suicide," Schlemiel observes that overcoming anxieties can either build or destroy a person. "Teenagers should communicate about their concerns and find creative solutions rather than try to handle things on their own," according to Schlemiel.

When you accept your worth, abilities and capabilities, it becomes irrelevant if other people have different opinions.

Even the most confident and extroverted people do have negative perception of themselves and they are also not totally satisfied. It's very normal to sometimes ponder over our choices, regret our actions, or an inherent desire to improve. Furthermore, when a person has an insecurity, he focuses more on his flaws identified by other persons rather than his accomplishments. Although insecurity is a common personality flaw and manifests differently in every individual, still it has one common feature: it frequently puts a great deal of stress on personal relationships.

3.1: Strengthen your bond with people who treat you well!

It's very difficult for teens to identify who is loyal to you and with whom you can develop a stronger relationship. That's why when a relationship gets stronger with the wrong person, who wants to see your insecurities instead of your talents, that's when the red flag pops up. You need to identify and accept them as soon as you can. Teens and adults should develop relationships with those people who always treat them well, who always motivate them and accept them with all their flaws. Those are the people who will bring most of the happiness and motivation in your life.

Those who mind don't matter, and those who matter don't mind, so be yourself and express whatever's on your mind.

Having best relationship with the people who appreciate you in any situation, allows you to share happiness throughout your life., which is one of the best qualities of them. However, one of the best aspects of having these people as close friends is having somebody to trust in when things are tough. You must have to be honest with people if you wish to build stronger relationships.

3.2: Public opinions are meant to be generic!

When I was in my teens, I was surprised to learn that negative opinions of people about me actually got glued to me and impacted my personal growth and I used to think that they didn't affect me. I still remember the schoolgirl who said,

"Stop acting like such a spoiled child." This is amongst my earliest memories of being attacked for something that wasn't even based on reality, yet I still thought what she said was correct about me. Without understanding or stopping to consider what "spoiled" actually meant, I spent a long time fighting to avoid becoming one. This proved true for all the other "bad" things I stopped doing with the hope of getting more acceptable to the rest of the world. But it never occurred. I was unable to achieve a place where I could satisfy everyone. I kept noticing indirect signals from others either pointing out my mistakes or directing me that what needs to be corrected.

Resultantly, I have had to deal with a lot of harassment in the workplace from colleagues during my adult life. Not only was I too afraid to defend myself, but I also had to suffer criticism in front of others. That's when I know I should not bother about these public opinions for myself. If I had not done that in the past, things would have been different.

Don't let the insecurities in other people's lives impact yours. There will always be someone who doesn't like you.

Among the most common insecurities in teens is the dilemma of social anxiety. Many people experience self-consciousness, anxiety and terror when sitting in front of others. It makes no difference if it's a gathering of coworkers or relatives. A deeply held feeling that you are unworthy of success is at the core of this fear. Believing that you are unimportant and incapable of making a meaningful contribution or that everything you say or act will be forever linked to you as a humiliation will only lower your self-worth and confidence.

3.3: Their outburst of insecurity on you is actually due to your strength!

Standing up for yourself, speaking out loud, having likes and dislikes and having confidence in your decision are the best things you can do for yourself. Your strength should be visible to others so that no one can take you for granted.

For example, if a female partner in a relationship stands for herself on something, that doesn't mean she is hurting her counterpart or does not care about him. Suppose she speaks about the things that she dislikes, it's genuinely her right to do so. If her partner does not understand this, it implies that he is the insecure one, not her. The insecurities that people have are just because you have that courage and strength which they don't like and are reluctant to accept establishing the fact that people's opinions should not matter.

Chapter 4: Pillar 3: "Self-Acceptance is a Selfless Act"

In the due course of time, we destroy ourselves from the inside when we don't accept who we are. Who will suffer when we compete against our own selves? Accepting that each of us has weaknesses and that everybody makes errors is necessary. Learning from mistakes should not be deemed as a negative experience that you should fully avoid. It's amongst the most effective ways to grow. Happiness and well-being depend solely on self-love. These qualities genuinely and visibly influence our personal, intellectual and mental well-being. When we reject to embrace who we are, we disconnect ourselves from the power that keeps us alive: our connection to the life eventually starts to break down due.

My mother frequently shares the story of my great grandma, who died when I was born. My great grandma was an independent woman, who used to manage a restaurant in addition to working as a maid to make her ends meet. She had 6 children and raising 6 kids is not an easy job as she was doing that with her work. Its only now that I can understand her feelings. Who wants to return home so exhausted to pass out as soon as they lay down. As a result of her excessive workload, she passed away due to cardiac failure while being at her job. She was never able to see her grandchild.

The greatest lesson I learned from her life was to take better care of myself and respect my values. No work, no family responsibilities, no commitments and no duties are worth sacrificing your wellbeing. In order to uphold both, my own values and that of my grandma's, who was never aware that she had the choice to do exactly the same, I learned self-love.

4.1: Love Yourself and Overcome its Obstacles

Imagine (for a moment while closing your eyes), spending every day of your life with a person who does not like you much and frequently makes derogatory statements about your education, beauty, abilities and future prospects. She is constantly there, watching you, causing you to feel uneasy and continually disapproving of you. Seriously, is that bad? Right? So many of us hear those voices in our heads. As a result, we always feel unsafe as we move around with this terrible voice speaking to us. These types of obstacles will be here for you throughout your entire life. It depends on you, how to overcome these obstacles by loving yourself and embracing your failures.

4.2: All Others Are Imperfect Too

I've been travelling for a while to reach to the point where I'm willing to accept my shortcomings and understand that would life really be significantly better without them! What would I be if I didn't have these flaws? I'd always be me, though. We all secretly aspire to perfection, perhaps because we believe that everyone else is flawless while we are really not, but the truth is that perfection lies in being flawed.

The presence of imperfections serves as a constant reminder that we are all in it together.

4.3: How to Develop Self-Acceptance?

At school, we are evaluated on the basis of our performance in exams, class discussions, assignments, field projects and in terms of how we fit in along with our classmates. All of this can support the science of acceptance and feelings of self-worth. Some of the many ways to develop self-acceptance are:

- ✓ *Try forgiving yourself*
- ✓ *Develop empathy for yourself*
- ✓ *Focus on being mindful*
- ✓ *Gratitude for your talents*
- ✓ *Set aside self-criticism*

Chapter 5: Pillar 4: "Never Let Someone Else Decide How Happy You Will be; Instead, Take Responsibility for Your Own Happiness"

You might have frequently realized that you needed somebody else to keep you happy. However, they haven't always met your expectations. No one blames them, though. Even when we are upset with them for not living up to our hopes for making us happy, we can't hold anyone else responsible. Many individuals are unaware that we are responsible for our own happiness. Nobody on this planet is meant to make others happy.

Your happiness depends on how you feel, not how others make you feel.

5.1: You Become What You Think

"You become what you believe" is among the most practical phrases. You need to manage your thoughts if you want to manage your personalities and your life. You must first recognize that you are a gem to yourself. Your mind was created to be a work of art. You can purposefully develop a life that is a gem for you if you are optimistic, prosperous, and possess creative thoughts. This work of art will appear differently to every one of us. We are all like artists who are in charge of making our own unique reality. Your life shouldn't be a carbon copy of anyone else's. Picasso's artwork differs significantly from Van Gogh's creation. Your life must be exclusive and represent your unique goals and aspirations.

5.2: Develop Sense of Gratitude

Being thankful encourages us to seek out and interact with the optimistic things in life while also boosting positive feelings like empathy and pleasure. This enables us to shift our focus away from negative feelings like anger and jealousy.

"Gratitude is a strong happiness booster."

You can develop gratitude habits by following these tips:

✓ *Be open-minded and grateful for everything.*
✓ *Recognize the goodness in your struggles.*
✓ *Write and maintain a gratitude notebook.*
✓ *Exhibit your feelings.*
✓ *Spend moments with family and friends.*

5.3: Give Yourself Positive Signals When in Dismay

Positive thoughts do not suggest overlooking life events. Positive thoughts involve an optimistic and constructive approach to bad situations. Even in the bad moments of your life, positive thinking has a lot of benefits. These are the tips you can use for thinking positively when facing dismay:

✓ *It's a chance to have a fresh start.*

✓ *I'll approach it from a unique perspective.*

- ✓ *I could not really fit it in. Well, I should review some of my goals.*
- ✓ *I'll do my best to make it happen.*
- ✓ *I'll try to do it once again.*

5.4: The Actual Steering is in Your Control

Expecting to become a positive person overnight is unrealistic if you tend to be hopeless. But over time, you'll become less critical of yourself and more supportive of who you are. You may also start to lose your sense of self-criticism. Being usually happy makes it easier for you to deal with stressful situations more positively. These abilities could be a factor in optimistic thinking. You just have to accept that you are the only one who really matters. Your thoughts, your decision, your achievements are just for you not for anyone else. With this perception, you can achieve anything in your practical life. Life is not about other people opinions, what they want you to become, or what they want from you. If you want to become a dancer, just go ahead or if you want to become a wrestler then just give it your 100 percent. Your life should just depend on your choices and decisions: not anyone else's.

Chapter 6: Pillar 5: "Fear is the Biggest Illusion of Them All"

We relate our emotional response to something that appears unsafe as being in fear. However, the term "fear" is also used to describe something that a person frequently feels terrible of.

When something or someone makes them feel insecure or unclear, people become afraid. As an illustration, a weak swimmer can be afraid of deep water. In this situation, the fear is beneficial since it warns the person to be cautious. If one could learn how to swim properly, they could get over their fear.

6.1: Fears and Failures Are Signs of Normality

Fear is a fundamental, natural feeling, much like happiness, sorrow and rage. It's a strong emotion we feel when something seems frightening or harmful. While you might not consider fear to be a good thing, it is an essential coping strategy. Fear makes us aware of possible danger and enables quick responses that keep us safe. Fortunately, you experienced your fear, else you may have not survived those circumstances. However, you could be thinking how well the human body responds to threats so rapidly and efficiently. The reason is that fear is a natural emotion. We have basic tendencies for survival.

"The lack of fear does not make someone brave. Having that fear while also identifying a solution to overcome it, is bravery."

6.2: Fears Usually Faced by Teenagers

When a teenager fears that their strategy, effort, or objective won't be successful, they develop a fear of failure. These anxieties are common, especially among teens who live or study in stressful surroundings. To some level, the fear of failing might encourage people to take proactive measures for ensuring their success. For instance, it might inspire a student to plan their assignments so they can finish everything on time. Some of the frequent fears that teens of today face, are:

- *Fear of being imperfect*
- *Fear of their parents being divorced*
- *Fear of failing in school*
- *Fear of not being enough*
- *Fear of rejection*

6.3: Overcoming Fears

Here are some tips which will help you to overcome these fears that scare you or makes you feel uncomfortable every day:

- *Take a short break from your busy life.*
- *Embrace your fears*
- *Visualize that the worst could happen*
- *Don't tend to be perfect every time*
- *Talk about your fears with your loved ones*

6.4: How to Stay Confident in Every Aspect of Your Life?

Terrible experiences can often harm self-confidence. We start doubting our own skills and have second thoughts about them. You may hear from your internal voice that you can't do anything. Perhaps you waste time in comparing yourself to the others, or perhaps you simply feel that you aren't living up to your full potential while having so much more to offer.

The great news is you can begin preparing the ground for establishing everlasting confidence right now!! You'll be more self-assured to accomplish your objectives if you have a clear sense of what your reason of living the life is! You are more open to new perspectives when you have confidence in your abilities. You experience less anxiety and are ready for the change you want in your life.

Chapter 7: Pillar 6"A Negative Mind Can Never Give You a Positive Life"

I would say that negative thoughts will result in a stressful and anxious life. You won't be happy about anything. No moment will be cherished. I won't claim that I never think of something negative. Certainly, I do. We just have to get through it. It will take some **patience** and **effort**. You can do everything in life with the help of these two things. The journey will be difficult though but each time a bad thought pops up into your head, you have to force yourself to keep positive.

7.1: Practice Positive Self-Talk

Your inner conversation is known as self-talk. It shows your emotions, opinions, problems and views which are controlled by your inner world. Positivity and negativity both exist in self-talk. It has the potential to be both inspiring and depressing. Your attitude influences how you talk to yourself a lot. Your self-talk may be more positive and cheerful if you are an optimistic. If you're normally pessimistic, the contrary is usually true. Optimist and positive thoughts can be used as powerful stress-reduction strategies. It is true that having a more optimistic attitude on life has some favorable effects on your health. A recent survey, found that optimistic people have a better standard of living.

7.2: Set Small Practical Goals and Celebrate Them

If your intention is to save money, your basic goal might be to collect $500 in 2 months. your next goal can be to stay healthy.

It might include taking 2 times walk a day or having two portions of vegetables each day for the following month. Dream large, but to begin, set the goal of taking one practical action that will bring you closer to your goal with each passing day. A real goal should be small and achievable. When you achieve the very first one, you can establish a new goal that will move you closer to your desire.

7.3: Count Your Perks Daily

Teenagers who participate in a variety of school activities, sporting events, voluntary work and academic interests typically have greater self-esteem. They have certain other things supporting their personality too, so they are not devastated by a failure in one field. When you do some productive activities, you should make a list of them in order to know that you have done something good that day.

7.4: Giving and Sharing is the Key

To establish and maintain friendships, play together, tell stories, and deal with rejection, you must understand how to share. Teenagers learn about cooperation and honesty via sharing. They discover that if they offer a small amount to others, they can also receive a small portion of what they want.

7.5: 7 Ways to Stop Negative Thoughts

Negative thoughts not only have bad effects on your practical life but also affect your emotional life. You can implement these steps to actually stop the negative thoughts:

- *Identify negative thoughts*
- *Confront your negative ideas*
- *Put your negative thoughts on hold*
- *Put your judgments aside*
- *Maintain gratitude*
- *Find professional assistance*
- *Think about your capabilities*

Chapter 8: Some FAQs and Experiences

8.1: Frequently Asked Questions and Confusions

Teenagers have a lot of questions and confusion in their minds related to self-esteem. Some questions really show their concerns. If you have such questions in your mind, you can identify your issue from these:

Am I feeling confused regarding the issues that are unrelated to me?

The fact that you are feeling so confused about some unrelated issues is because you are overthinking everything in your life. Overthinking just makes you feel inferior from others. Just focus on the things which are really important. Don't give a thought to those things which don't have any significant value.

Am I making assumptions too soon?

This is the effect of believing strongly on the weak evidences. Depressed people frequently believe that others are judging them. But none of them can read your mind. We don't know what other people are thinking about us. So, we should not waste our time in making assumptions.

Am I raising queries which are unanswerable?

This is the most common question among teens. Mostly teens ask questions to themselves which really have no answer. It's because they think about one thing over and over again and eventually, they start to doubt their decisions. You should not waste your time on these questions. And if you stop raising these questions you will witness a positive change in your life.

Am I concentrating on my weakness and forgetting my strengths?

When people become depressed, they often overlook the problems they handled successfully in the past, and resources that can help them to overcome current difficulties. Once they succeed to change their thinking pattern, they are often amazed by their own ability to deal with problems.

8.2: The Success Stories

Let me tell you some success stories for your motivation:

1. I had a friend in my university days. Her name was Alice. She had a lot of self-esteem issues in her early teens. Her father was a very depressed man who always demotivated and discouraged her. He never appreciated her, although she was the topper of her class. Because of him, she lost a lot of her confidence. On the other hand, her mother was a very kind soul. She loved and appreciated her as much as she desired for. And just because of her, she was able to trust herself and enhance her confidence to build her self-esteem as a whole.

2. My roommate, Jane told me her story. She had a severe self-esteem issue having no plan for her life. Girls used to dislike her in school because of her weird personality. She used to live in the suburbs, in a community in which girls usually don't have any dreams related to their careers. Because of the frequent move, she missed the school a lot and eventually couldn't pursue her studies. When she got married, she

became dependent on her husband. But sadly, after two years, her husband died in a car accident. She was left alone in this mean world. with a baby boy then. She didn't know what she would do to give her boy a good life. She shared her story to one of her best-friend who motivated her and advised her to trust her own self, by starting with baby steps. Then, she started thinking about this in her own mind over and over again and gradually started to trust her decisions. One day she came up with an idea to start a small food catering business. She trusted her abilities and talents. Now, she successfully runs her business and has a restaurant of her own. She is giving herself and her boy a good lifestyle, which she always wanted.

Conclusion

Since you have your self-esteem with you in any scenario, including school, gatherings, friendships, interviews and dinner parties, it is among the most significant determinants of how you will handle every detail of your life. You have such a better rate of success and enjoyment in all you do, once you have a strong level of self-worth.

If you have self-esteem, you can seek support when you don't know something in class. Since you are aware that you are not a loser and that you only need to put forth more effort, it helps you to recover after receiving a poor rating. Considering your school or professional goals provide you the courage to pursue your passions and take practical actions to accomplish your goals. When you have balanced self-esteem, you may continue moving forward in your academic life by concentrating on your successes rather than your flaws.

The entire family's happiness improves when family relations are defined by good self-esteem. A strong sense of self-worth enables you to bear the restrictions your family or even other relatives impose on you without feeling insulted. It enables you to establish and communicate your own opinions in a mature manner, rather than acting immaturely and over sensitively. Even though you do not often agree with a family member's actions, it allows you to appreciate the positive aspects of each one. Appreciation for varying perspectives and respectful and honest conversation are all influenced and regulated by a healthy self-esteem which results in strengthening the ties among family and friends.